GOD INSPIRED POETRY

FINDING RICHES IN THE ORDINARY

BARBARA KAREN HODGES

Purpose Publishing
1503 Main Street #168
Grandview, Missouri 64030
www.PurposePublishing.com

Finding Riches in the Ordinary
Copyright © 2021 by Barbara Karen Hodges
ISBN: 979-8-7001762-2-4

For permission requests, write to the publisher, addressed "Attention: Permissions Coordinator," at the address above.

Bulk Ordering Information: Quantity sales. Special discounts are available on quantity purchases by groups, churches, ministry associations, and others. For details to reach out and contact the author at writerink59@yahoo.com.

Scriptures used in this book are from the King James Version and Amplified Versions of the Bible.
Printed in the United States of America.

Dedication

Finding riches in the ordinary,

that is what I like to do.

The poems, anecdotes, and reflections,

are my gifts to you.

Many family and friends,

have encouraged me along the way.

The Holy Spirit has given me,

the various words to say.

There is something about the ordinary,

that catches my eyes.

Looking beyond the surface,

can reveal a surprise.

Riches in the ordinary mean more,

than silver or gold.

Take time, yourself, and see,

what the ordinary will unfold.

Table of Contents

Riches in the Ordinary

There are riches in the ordinary,

I have come to realize,

as I open my heart,

and also, my eyes.

Birds chirping in the morning,

or the moon shining at night.

These things and more,

fill me with delight.

There was a gray squirrel,

running all about.

He scampered away,

when he heard the neighbor shout.

I saw a friend,

I had not seen in a while.

We spent time catching up,

in the produce aisle.

Yes, there are riches in the ordinary,

I look around to see,

there are untold blessings,

and all are absolutely free.

I use my senses,

finding riches along the way,

discovering the unexpected,

and how it makes my day.

Psalm 118:24

This is the day the Lord has made; let us rejoice and be
glad in it.

I started cleaning out a closet one day. As I was pulling items out, I found a brand-new jigsaw puzzle. Several years earlier, during a difficult season, I started doing puzzles. Somehow this one never got done. This was the perfect time to begin. It took me two weeks. As I was putting the last pieces in place, the Lord gave me this poem.

Puzzle Fun

Putting a puzzle together is so much fun,

A bit of a challenge, but a beautiful one.

There are numerous pieces of colors and shapes.

Some of the scenery may be lovely landscapes.

Do I start with the borders,

Or sort colors into piles?

Do I follow puzzle rules,

Or create my own styles?

It is exciting when pieces fit together,

Especially sooner rather than later.

When a piece fits into place,

A smile comes slowly across your face.

Our lives are a puzzle, so it seems to us

God fits the pieces together,

When in Him we trust.

Are there pieces in your life,

That are puzzling to you?

Be patient, follow Him,

Watch to see what He will do.

Circumstances may happen,

We do not understand.

We must have faith,

God has us in His Hand.

Proverbs 3:5-6

Trust in the Lord with all your heart, and do not rely
on your own understanding: in all your ways know
Him and He will make your paths straight.
What puzzle pieces of life are you trying to fit
together?

Talk it over with the Lord.

As I looked out my living room window, in a matter of a few minutes, four different trucks drove down my street. They were busy making deliveries. Our nation was experiencing a pandemic. People were shopping online at a higher rate. For some reason, this flurry of activity caught my attention. I stood at the window for a few more minutes. I started looking around and noticed the red flowering bush in my neighbor's yard and the lack of much traffic. What really stood out was the absence of people. Not even any children were outside playing. It was a beautiful day too. This is the backdrop for the following poem.

What Do You See?

I am looking out the window,

And what do I see?

Three different truck companies making deliveries.

The mail carrier is also on the street.

None of these companies are missing a beat.

The friendly blue skies seem quieter too.

There have not been many airplanes to view.

My neighbor has a beautiful red bush.

After a rain, it is even more lush.

A car or two may come and go.

Living on a cul-de-sac limits the flow.

I have not seen anyone walking today,

Not even children trying to play.

The sound of a lawnmower is loud and clear.

But right now, that is all I hear.

As you look out your window,

What do you see?

Are there any signs of God's creativity?

Genesis 1:31
God saw all that He had made, and it was very good
indeed.
When was the last time you saw the hand of God in
your life?

I was with a group of teachers on a warm summer day. We were participating in a writing marathon at our local zoo. We went off in different directions. Our goal was to get inspired by our observations and write. After a period of time, we met back together and shared our writings.

The Zoo: A Special Place

It took a lot of planning,

To put this zoo together.

Families love to visit here,

Especially in great weather.

There are many different habitats,

For every living thing,

From the largest gray elephant,

To the smallest birds that sing.

Rock formations, waterfalls,

And clear cool streams,

Delight the visitor's eyes,

And is a naturalist's dream.

There are a variety of jobs here,

That need to be done,

Whether by many,

Or only by one.

The animals must be cared for,

Fed, and checked,

While the grounds must be monitored,

And very well kept.

The zoo is an awesome place,

On any given day.

The staff who work there,

Makes sure it stays that way.

It is exciting to know,

There is such a place,

That can put a smile on every face.

Psalm 104: 24

How countless are your works, Lord! In wisdom You
have made them all; the earth is full of your
creatures.

Where is your favorite place to spend time with the
Lord?

As far back as I can remember, I have always loved writing letters. It was even more delightful when I received one in return. Over the years I continued this practice. I even made sure I used pretty postage. That just added a special uniqueness. Receiving a letter from an old friend gave me the inspiration for these words.

A Letter is a Gift

A letter is a special gift,

To pass along the way,

Whether you have much

Or little to say.

Seeing a letter among the bills,

Is such a welcomed treat.

Knowing someone has thoughts

Of you is so sweet.

Sit right down with

Some paper and pen.

Write that letter

To a family member or friend.

Imagine the smile a letter

From you will bring.

It will be worth

The stamp and time,

To do such a thing.

Proverbs 16:24

Pleasant words are a honeycomb: sweet to the
taste and health to
the body.

When was the last time you shared some pleasant
words?

Has anyone sent you some sweet words lately?

.

The last few years I have learned to be intentional. What do I mean? I have stopped taking things for granted. Each day I am determined to see the Lord's hand in my daily moments. This has led me to have a more grateful heart and to see He really is in control. What a relief it is not to carry weight that is not mine to carry.

On the Lookout

Are you seeing what God is doing?

He is always faithful and pursuing.

The Father loves to bless His child.

He often does it in Heavenly style.

Are you aware throughout each day,

How only the Lord can make a way?

He delights in showing us His glory.

All He does adds to our story.

Be thankful God's love is everlasting.

He never gets tired of us asking.

The things He wants from us,

Include obedience, love, and trust.

Be on the lookout during the day,

To see God's handiwork on display.

Psalm 33:22

May your faithful love rest on us, Lord, for we put
our trust in you.

Is there something new you have noticed? What is
something you may have been taking for granted
that you could thank God for?

There is something refreshing about saying thank you after someone has shown kindness. Think how much more important to say thank you to the Lord. Being thankful is especially important to God. All throughout the Bible He reminds His people to give thanks, no matter the circumstances.

A Heart of Gratitude

Count your many blessings.

You have several, I am sure.

As you think about them,

You will remember more.

Thank the Lord for each of them,

No matter the size.

Some of them are easy to see,

While others may be in disguise.

Giving thanks in all things,

Is the way we do our part.

Doing so on a regular basis,

Delights the Father's heart.

Count your many blessings,

Day in and day out.

This is what being thankful,

Is really all about.

Psalm 136:1

Give thanks to the Lord, for He is good. His faithful
love endures forever.

I Thessalonians 5:17

Give thanks in everything; for this is God's will for
you in Christ Jesus.

Make a list of people, things, or circumstances you
are thankful for.

I was slicing some tomatoes to add to my garden salad of lettuce, carrots, and cucumbers. At the same moment I was back in time sitting in my grandfather's garden. Oh, he was so proud of his masterpiece. This was a collaboration in the highest sense. He knew it was the Lord who blessed his efforts. Every year something new would be added. Family and neighbors were always the recipients of his bounty.

I could recall the unique flavor of a red, juicy, plump tomato. This was pure bliss and redefined the meaning of fresh. I do not know why memories like this come flooding back over us when we least expect them. But as I ate my salad that day, I could not help but have a satisfied smile on my face. I thought of my grandfather. I am sure he is on the gardening team in Heaven and having a wonderful time.

Ecclesiastes 3:1-2

There is an occasion for everything, a time to plant and a time to uproot.

Notes

Early fall is my favorite time of year. The trees are beginning to change in appearance, football games are underway, and our clothing selections become more in tune with the cooler temperatures. Our taste buds also get into the spirit of autumn. That first slice of apple pie with a dollop of ice cream leaves a delicious memory behind. Yes, autumn is a favorite time of the year for me.

Autumn Days

I enjoy autumn days,

So very much.

The gentle wind,

The colorful leaves,

Are signs of the Master's touch.

I see robins, gray squirrels,

A rabbit here and there.

The animals all know,

There is a change in the air.

What changes are you noticing,

In your life today?

Whatever they are,

Father God will guide your way.

Look to Him for wisdom,

Giving Him thanks as you go.

His promises are true,

As we already know.

James 1:17

Every good and perfect gift is from above, coming
down from the Father of lights, who does not
change like shifting shadows.

Isn't it comforting to know that even though good
and bad changes take place, we can count on God
to be the same all the time?

I have some family members who are in the middle of some upsetting circumstances. My concern for them has caused many sleepless nights. I really did not want to be involved, but emotionally I cannot distance myself from them. Turning the matter over to the Lord is the only way I can handle the weight.

A Hard Place

Are you in a hard place right this minute?

Are you asking yourself how did I get in it?

Is a loved one's issue tugging at your heart?

Do you feel that it is tearing you apart?

We all need the armor of God for protection,

to ward off the enemy's bullets of deception.

It is a constant battle, twenty-four seven,

Some answers won't be seen this side of heaven.

In the meantime, it is a daily fight.

We must be praying morning, noon, and at night.

Ephesians 6:11, 16

Put on the full armor of God so that you can stand against the schemes of the devil... In every situation take up the shield of faith with which you can extinguish all the flaming arrows of the evil one.

Meditate on the armor of God. Is there a part of the armor you may need to shore up?

We each have a responsibility to model Jesus to anyone we meet. This is especially important when there are children in our lives. Whether we are parents, grandparents, aunts, uncles, educators, or anyone else, we need to be great role models. Children are precious in God's sight.

Children: Pieces of God's Heart

Each child comes to us as a piece of God's heart.

He will give us what we need so we can do our part.

Taking care of children is not an easy task.

But wisdom is available if only we would ask.

The Lord loves our children and

knows what they need.

We are to love and teach them,

God's words to heed.

Take time to listen before we speak.

Hear what is on their minds

for it is our ears they seek.

Teach the children to obey God in what they do,

Day in and day out, their whole lives through.

It is obedience that thrills the Father's heart.

Teach them this right from the start.

As adults we are God's children too.

His grace is sufficient for what we need to do.

He promises to be with us every step of the way.

We should take time to sit at His feet each day.

3 John 1:4

I have no greater joy than this: to hear that my
children are walking in truth.

When was the last time you modeled Jesus around
a young person?

How did you do it?

A Lesson from a Squirrel

I was looking out my kitchen window one morning. There were some squirrels having a grand old time. They were scampering all around the yard. One squirrel caught my attention. I zeroed in on him just to see what he would do. What I observed that morning gave me ideas on how to improve my walk with the Lord.

•The squirrel went from spot to spot researching the area. When I am reading the scriptures, do I do research to further my understanding?

•When the squirrel found something of interest, it sniffed at it for a moment. It was if he was deciding to stay or move on. Do I meditate on a verse or do I quickly move on to the next one?

•Bingo! The squirrel has hit upon something. He sits there with sustained interest.

Do I find myself so wrapped up in the scriptures that I camp out there for a while, excited about new revelation?

•I tapped on the window to get his attention. Did he drop what was in his mouth? Not at all. He held on to it and ran off in another direction. Do I let myself get distracted or do I hold on to what the Holy Spirit shows me?

Watching the squirrels gave me a new energy to fine tune the way I approach my time in the Bible. I need to come to my quiet time with the expectation that I will find nuggets of truth each time. Nuggets that will carry me through each day.

Genesis 1:25

So God made the wildlife of the earth according to their kinds, the livestock according to their kinds, and all the creatures that crawl on the ground according to their kinds. And God saw that it was good.

Prayer is talking to our Father. Having regular conversations with Him. Are you aware of how often you pray? One day I purposely took notice of my prayer times. Asking the Lord to forgive me for some ill thought or deed, interceding for family, friends, or even strangers, and laying out personal requests took up the content of my prayers.

It seemed that the more I prayed, the more things came to mind to pray about. As I spent time in prayer throughout the day, I was more aware of God's presence, my environment, and the people whose paths I came across.

For example, when I heard sirens, I stopped to pray for all the people who may have been affected by the circumstances. When I had a poor attitude about something, I quickly sought forgiveness. Seeing the various shades of green on the trees and bushes made me have a new appreciation for the beauty God provides. Having a lifestyle of prayer brings a person closer to the Lord.

Psalm 66:18

If I had been aware of malice in my heart, the Lord
would not have listened.

I Thessalonians 5:17, 18

Pray constantly, give thanks in everything; for this is
God's will for you in Christ Jesus.

Philippians 4:6

Don't worry about anything, but in everything
through prayer and petition with thanksgiving,
present your requests to God. .

It has been said that the Bible is God's love letter to us. If only we took that more seriously, what a better world we would have. His Word tells us how to love. He shows us how to love one another. He tells us that we cannot love Him who we have not seen and hate our brother (sister) whom we do see. It does not take much to show love. It is all in our actions.

Love Message

Here is a love message,

Just for you.

Letting you know,

Someone cares today,

And the whole year through.

It is always time to show love,

To those we are around,

Offering a warm smile,

And not wearing a frown.

Encourage someone,

Making their day,

Either by something you do,

Or something you say.

1 John 4:7-8, 19

Dear friends, let us love one another, because love is from God, and everyone who loves has been born of God and knows God... The one who does not love does not know God, because God is love... We love because He first loved us.

Spend time today basking in the Father's love for you.

Turn on some worship music and praise God for who he is.

Just thinking about having a picnic brings sweet memories to mind. It can be as simple as a sandwich, apple, a cookie, and drink. Or it could be a full-blown cookbook picnic complete with a red checkered tablecloth and a wicker picnic basket. Whatever way the picnic turns out, giving thanks to the Father adds a special flavor to the day.

A Picnic Lunch

Potato salad, fruit salad,

some coleslaw too,

Along with fried chicken

and a biscuit to chew.

Pretty cotton napkins, forks,

knives, and spoons,

Setting the table to eat around noon.

Oh, what did I forget,

let me think.

I remember now,

an icy cold drink.

A picnic lunch gives

the day a spark,

No matter if it is at home

or at the local park.

Psalm 118: 24

This is the day the Lord has made; let us rejoice and
be glad in it.

Now, plan to have a picnic sometime soon.

Isn't it amazing the many, many stars that can be seen on a clear night? I was outside on such a night and one star was shining so brightly. I thought about the star the wise men followed to find Jesus. It was a moment to give thanks to the Father.

A Special Star

There was a special star,

Shining long ago.

It gave the earth,

A heavenly glow.

The wise men used it,

As their guide,

Traveling to be,

By Jesus' side.

Their hearts were full,

Of wonder and joy.

There was something unique,

About this baby boy.

Jesus grew in wisdom,

Stature, and favor.

He was born to be,

Our Lord and Savior.

That star is still shining,

So very bright.

As it did on that wonderful,

Glorious night.

Matthew 2:1-2

After Jesus was born in Bethlehem of Judea in the
days of King Herod, wise men from the east arrived
in Jerusalem saying, "Where is he who has been
born king of the Jews? For we saw his star at its
rising and have come to worship him."

On the next clear night, think about that special
event that took place many years ago.

For some reason I woke up extra early this morning. I realized the birds outside my window were chirping away. They were so loud. Suddenly the chirping stopped. I waited for it to start again. Nothing. Strange, I thought. I googled on the Internet, Why did the birds suddenly stop chirping? The answer discussed the possibility of a predator or a human getting too close. Whatever the reason, it gave me pause to remember that even the birds can remind us of the Lord's presence in our day.

An Early Morning Reminder

The birds were chirping,

This morning loud and clear,

Letting me know that God is near.

A wonderful reminder that He is in charge,

And can handle our fears, whether small or large.

I am glad I could hear the birds sing,

It is like God is saying, I got this thing.

Pay attention throughout your day,

Seeing that God is leading the way.

We are in this together, you and me,

Find ways to act responsibly.

The Lord wants our attention, there is no doubt,

We need His wisdom to figure things out.

As we are learning to cope,

Look to Jesus, our only hope.

Psalm 104:12

The birds of the sky live beside the springs; they
make their voices heard among the foliage.

Remember how the Father provides for the birds.
He has promised to take care of us. What concerns
do you need to give to him today?

We are living in unsettling times. People need encouragement. It does lift the spirit when one hears encouraging words. Children as well as adults need to have life giving words spoken over and to them. Watch how someone's posture goes from a slump to a rising up. Positive words are like medicine.

Be an Encourager

We all need encouragement

During our days,

Circumstances come

Against us

In so many ways.

It makes daily life much easier

When we encourage one another,

The Holy Spirit can give us

What we can give each other.

A word spoken here

Or a friendly smile,

May be just what someone needs

To go that next mile.

The impact of our encouragement

We may never know,

But pointing someone to Jesus

Is the way to go.

As we get encouragement

From the Father

Let us be loving encouragers

To each other.

I Thessalonians 5:11
Therefore encourage one another and build each
other up as you are already doing.

Memorize a verse about encouragement.

What a different world we would have if we carried a small amount of concern for one another. Being available is something we all can do. It would be contagious if we saw kindness, generosity, respect, or humility on display.

Being There

Shoulder to shoulder we need to stand,

Being available to offer a hand.

Bear one another's burden, the Bible does say.

What can we do as we go our way?

Stay connected and support one another,

For in the Lord, we are sisters and brothers.

When we are blessed, we are to be a blessing too.

For the Lord has things He wants us to do.

We might need to go that extra mile,

Or give someone we meet a much-needed smile.

Let us open our eyes so we will see,

All the endless possibilities.

Galatians 6:2, 10

Carry one another's burdens; in this way you will fulfill the law of Christ... Therefore, as we have opportunity, let us work for the good of all, especially for those who belong to the household of faith.

Have you ever had a moment when you felt God did something special just for you? I was on my way home. I looked up at the sky and caught my breath. It was an absolutely beautiful shade of blue. There was not a cloud to be found. This was one of those personal moments between the Lord and me. I pulled off to the side of the road so I could take it all in. I felt the Lord's love that day. This poem reflects that moment.

Blue Sky

Did you see the sky today?

It really took my breath away.

The shade of blue was an awesome sight.

There were no clouds of puffy white.

Why did this sky stand out to me?

The Lord opened my eyes

So I would see.

It was something special

That could not be undone.

He did it for me, an audience of one.

What is the Father showing you?

I am sure there is something

If you look too.

Psalm 19:1

The heavens declare the glory of God, and the
expanse proclaims the work of His hands.

Go outside today and look at the sky. What do you
see? Do the same at night. Praise the Lord for His
creation.

Don't you love butterflies? Seeing them fly about on a summer day, brings a smile to my face. They are like receiving little surprises at any given moment. Every summer I think about getting some flowers that will attract butterflies. So far, I have not gotten any since they seem to appear on their own. But one day…

Butterflies

Bits of color flying about,

Can be seen often, day in and day out.

Butterflies' wings are dainty and light,

Enabling them to move swiftly, out of our sight.

Their colors are awesome to behold,

From various shades of blue and

Green, to a bright gold.

What treats they are for my eyes.

I love thanking the Lord,

For such a delightful surprise.

Revelations 4:11

Our Lord and God, you are worthy to receive glory and honor and power, because you have created all things, and by your will they exist and were created.

Name some of God's creations you enjoy.

Whenever there has been a disaster, people are quick to respond. During the Christmas holidays there are myriads of gift drives to make sure people on rough times have a happy holiday. These events are noteworthy. I wonder what impact it would make if each of us intentionally looked for ways to show we care on a regular basis, not just certain times during the year.

Caring

Have you been a caring person today?

If someone is upset, do you know what to say?

If someone falls, will you help her up?

If she needs a drink, will you offer a cup?

If someone has a need you can fill,

Will you act or just sit still?

Have you been a caring person today?

Did you ask someone if she wants to pray?

Sometimes it may be only you

To remind someone what God can do.

As you go along your way,

Be that caring person today.

Matthew 25:40

And the King will answer them, "Truly I tell you, whatever you did for one of the least of these brothers and sisters of mine, you did for me."

Name some ways you can be intentional in showing you care.

Do you save your calendars or date books from year to year? I did not realize how many I had saved until recently. I was amazed at the gold mine of information held within those monthly pages. It is interesting to go back in time and revisit the events via memories. There were birthdays, funerals, picnics, graduations, medical appointments, bill due dates, and on and on. These calendars are part of my history.

They also revealed how I used my time. The older calendars reflected my roles as a mom and teacher, while the newer calendars reflect my older years. There were play dates, dentist appointments, school activities, and scouting events, just to name a few. The newer calendars highlighted more doctor appointments, but this time for me, Grandma. After retirement, the dates on the calendar were influenced by activities at church

One major thread that ran through all those calendars were birthday dates. I had an aunt who always remembered everyone's birthday. You may not have gotten cards from anyone else, but you could always count on getting one from Aunt Mary. I have tried to do that as well. But I was no match for her. She had this tradition fined tuned.

Something else I had written on those calendars were goals. I found that if I wrote a goal down, the more likely I would reach it. One of the goals I had noted was to write one letter a week for that month. I recorded my efforts. I did miss one week, but I believe the three that I did write could be counted as a success. Otherwise, they may not have gotten written.

There were also answered prayer notations throughout the pages, as well as prayers still waiting to be answered. All in all, having these nuggets of history gave me an opportunity to see how the Lord has been with me over the years.

Psalm 143:5

I remember the days of old; I meditate on all you
have done; I reflect on the work of your hands.
If you have a calendar or date book, peruse through
it, and see what you learn about yourself.

What can you give thanks or praise God for?

I was watching television one afternoon. One commercial after another was trying to tell me what I needed. It was either a certain toothpaste for whiter teeth, a new and improved laundry detergent for brighter looking clothes, or a food service that would deliver fresh meals so I would never have to cook again. I started thinking about other things someone might need.

Everybody Needs..........

Everybody needs a dollar.

A dollar can buy an ice cream cone.

Everybody needs a star.

It will smile at you during the night.

Everybody needs a sponge.

It can soak up the sad moments.

Everybody needs a quiet time.

It helps to settle us down.

Everybody needs to see a rainbow.

It gives us hope for another day.

Everybody needs another dollar,

To buy an ice cream cone for a friend.

Philippians 4:19

And my God will supply all your needs according to his riches in glory in Christ Jesus.

What is a need in your life right now? As you look around, do you see a need you could fill?

I was at the cemetery with my daughter and son-in-law. We were there to make burial arrangements for his mom. She had fought a valiant battle with cancer. While discussing the arrangements, I noticed this little bird was just sitting nearby. With people so close, I thought it would fly away, but it did not. Somehow, the little bird's presence was a sign of comfort.

A Feathered Friend

Little bird, why were you with us at the cemetery?

You did not fly away as most birds

would have done.

You sat right there and watched us.

We finished making burial arrangements.

You then flew away.

It was as though you were overseeing the plans.

Little bird, thank you for being there.

Somehow you gave us a sweet peace.

John 14: 27

Peace I leave with you. My peace I give to you. I do not give to you as the world gives. Don't let your heart be troubled or fearful.

Peace in one's heart is priceless. Is there something stealing your peace today? Spend time talking to God about it.

"I am praying for you." These are some of the kindest words a friend could say. Just hearing those words can lift one's spirit very quickly. They may not lessen the pain or sorrow. But it does allow you to experience some light in an otherwise dark moment.

Not long ago I ran into an old friend. She is one of those people that I may not see very often, but when I do, it is easy to pick up from where we left off. At that time I had shared something what was heavy on my heart. I did not intend to share, but the words started to flow. I now know that was one of God's divine appointments. Several weeks later, we ran into each other again. The first thing she said to me was those five powerful little words, "I am praying for you." She had taken my burden and had come to the Father's throne of grace on my behalf. Hearing her say those words lifted my spirit more than anything else could have at that moment.

There have been a few times I have shared what was on my heart and really had no idea if I had been heard. When my friend told me about her prayer, I was humbled. The Apostle Paul was always encouraging the believers to pray for one another and for him too. My friend was a Paul to me that day.

As I reflected on that encounter, I thought about my own prayer life. Have I been as faithful to pray for others? Did I hear an unspoken prayer request? How many opportunities have I missed in coming before the throne of grace for someone else? I must confess, I am on the ball when there is a crisis. It is when everything is going well that I have dropped the ball. That is human nature. No excuse—Scripture reminds me that I have a new nature, the mind of Christ.

Is the Lord bringing someone to mind as you read these words? Pray for that person right now. I don't mean the generic "God bless everyone" type of prayer. Be specific. Then if you meet that person one day, encourage her heart as my friend encouraged me by saying, "I am praying for you."

Spring is one of my favorite seasons. It is a time of newness. God's creativity is on display. The earth does appear to be waking up from its long winter nap. The birds are singing their songs, while squirrels and rabbits scamper about. Buds on the trees are poking out their heads while the flowers are also making an appearance.

Spring is Here!

Hip, hip, hooray is our cheer!

Smiles on our faces

Because Spring is here.

The earth is waking up

From its winter nap,

With no concerns

About a cold weather snap.

The trees are budding

And plants are sprouting.

The weather is lovely

For a nice outing.

Birds can be heard

Singing their tunes,

While the flowers begin

To burst forth in blooms.

Lawns are turning

From brown to green.

Rabbits and squirrels

Can often be seen.

Oh yes, Spring is here,

We are happy to say.

Thank You, Father God,

For this beautiful day.

Solomon 2:11-12

For now the winter is past; the rain has ended and
gone away. The blossoms appear in the
countryside. The time of singing has come, and the
turtledove's cooing is heard in our land.

What changes are you noticing outside today?

Flying has not been high on my list. I have a fear. Since I live hundreds of miles from my hometown, traveling by airplane is the best way to go. On this flight, I started saying some of my favorite verses to calm myself. As we began to lift off, a new feeling swept over me. As the airplane rose higher and higher, it was like the Spirit of God took over. I had a peace I never experienced before. I can honestly say that for the first time, I was enjoying the flight.

From the Airplane Window

Up, up in the air we go,

Leaving behind the things below.

White puffy clouds scattered about,

Created by Father God, there is no doubt.

The higher we go, the more clouds I see.

This massive blue sky overwhelms me.

I am so glad God is in control.

That is the only way peace flooded my soul.

Are you up in the air about something today?

Cast it on Jesus as He makes a way.

Colossians 3:2

Set your mind on things above, not on earthly things.

Isaiah 26: 3

You will keep the mind that is dependent on you in perfect peace, for it is trusting in you.

What has you up in the air today? Are there clouds hiding God's presence?

One of my grandsons called me recently. He checks in periodically. Since he lives in a different state, we do not see each other very often. On this call, I could hear frustration in his voice. He is usually upbeat. I asked him what was going on. He said he was restless; nothing was working out like he thought. I gave him some words of encouragement. He thanked me and promised to stay in touch and give me updates as he continued his journey to discover what was next.

Frustration

I can hear the frustration

In your voice,

Perceiving that you have no choice.

In your mind time is slipping away.

You wonder if you will

Find your way.

You have dreams,

Wanting to taste success,

But continually feeling

A sense of unrest.

All is not lost.

There is much to gain.

A relationship with Christ

Will keep you sustained.

Ask the Father

To guide you each day.

He will show you a more excellent way.

The Lord knows you inside and out.

A relationship with Him is what it is all about.

He really wants to hear your voice.

You will soon realize

You do have a choice:

Will I continue doing things my way,

Or will I do what I hear Him say?

Getting into the scriptures daily is key.

That is how He talks to you and to me.

Galatians 6:9

Let us not get tired of doing good, for we will reap
at the proper time if we don't give up.

Have you ever been tempted to give up on a
dream?

Share your frustration with a close friend and pray
together for the Lord's guidance.

Notes

I was on my way to work one morning. It had rained during the night, so the ground was soft. When I passed the park, a gaggle of geese were milling around a patch of ground. I guess worms were in plenty supply since the ground was quite wet. I smiled just imagining the enjoyment the geese were having that morning.

A Gaggle of Geese

I drove past the park today,

And saw many geese.

Since the ground was wet,

They were enjoying a wormy feast.

Ten or more were getting,

Their fill that day.

Those worms better look out,

And try to crawl away.

It was fun watching,

Those feathered friends strut about.

One goose had a large worm,

Dangling from its mouth.

Will they be there tomorrow,

Or will they fly away?

I hope I will see them,

On another day.

Matthew 6: 25-26

Therefore I tell you: Don't worry about your life or what you will eat; or what you will drink; or about your body, what you will wear. Isn't life more than food and the body more than clothing? Consider the birds of the sky: They don't sow or reap or gather into barns, yet your heavenly Father feeds them. Aren't you worth more than they?

Meditate on these verses to remind yourself Who is your provider.

When a person is going through a difficult season, it is sometimes hard to see the Lord at work. It is when one gets on the other side of that season that things can be more clearly seen. As healing continues to take place, there has been plenty of evidence to show me how God has been and continues to be faithful. A person needs to be intentional on looking to see how God is being faithful.

God is Faithful

God does heal the brokenhearted.

I have found this to be true.

He takes away my sorrow

And makes all things new.

I am not the person I use to be.

While learning about Jesus,

I am learning about me.

Healing is coming day after day.

It is the Holy Spirit

who is paving my way.

This is very comforting to know,

Keeping my eyes on things above,

Not on the things below.

Lamentations 3:22-23

Because of the Lord's faithful love we do not perish,
for his mercies never end. They are new every
morning; great is your faithfulness.

What areas in your life have you witnessed
evidence of God's faithfulness?

I am always amazed how clean the environment looks after a rain. The colors are so bright and fresh. The bushes in my front yard are examples of different shades of green. Those in the sun look much differently than the ones in the shade. The cardinal's red color is so alive and bright. Even the brown spots in the yard look fresher. The Lord is indeed the master artist.

God's Palette

After a rain what do I see?

Shades of green on many trees.

Our Lord has a palette of vibrant colors.

He shares them with me and many others.

It is amazing how rain cleans the air.

We are able to see what was always there.

God spreads the colors all around,

From the birds in the sky to the flowers on the ground.

Appreciate the Lord's artistry from day to day.

Give thanks to Him whenever you pray.

Open your eyes and take it all in.

As the rain cleans the earth,

Jesus' blood has cleansed our sin.

Jeremiah 14:22

Can any of the worthless idols of the nations bring rain? Or can the skies alone give showers? Are you not the Lord our God? We therefore put our trust in you, for you have done all these things.

Next time it rains, take note of what you notice about your surroundings. Give thanks to the Lord for His artwork.

Several years ago, I wanted to write a book. I had gone through an extremely hard season and wanted to capture the feelings and lessons I experienced. As I began this journey, I ran into obstacles that gave me pause. Nothing was falling into place. This went on for quite a long time. I finally decided to stop and put the project on hold. Periodically I would try again with the same results. Several years later, circumstances began to come together and there was a flow I had not experienced before. The following poem is part of that journey.

God's Timing

"It is all in the timing,"

We have heard people say.

But I am learning God has His own way.

I started a project,

And nothing went right.

I was getting frustrated

And feeling uptight.

Forcing an outcome is not very wise.

I put the project away with a heavy sigh.

Over the years I would try now and then,

But still it did not work once again.

Almost out of the blue,

That project began to take shape.

I could feel a smile coming over my face.

It was God's timing there is no doubt.

There was nothing difficult to figure out.

Now I know patience is the key,

Relying on the Lord's timetable for me.

It is all in God's timing. Unless the Lord is in something, we are wasting our time and energy. Wait on Him to open the doors. His way is perfect.

Lamentations 3:25-26

The Lord is good to those who wait for Him, to the person who seeks Him. It is good to wait quietly for salvation from the Lord.

A four-letter word that we all need to have on the tip of our tongue is hope. This word is small but mighty. When hope is in one's heart, there is an extra amount of strength that rises. Conversely, when hope is gone, life takes on a different hue. Our hope can only be found in the Lord. Draw close to Him.

Hope

I am looking out the window

At the snow-covered ground.

I am looking for evidence

That God is still around.

The daily news is full

Of violence, corruption, and such.

People are looking all over

For signs of His touch.

I am watching a gray squirrel

Scampering to and fro.

It has hope of finding,

Food hidden in the snow.

Hope, that is what we need too.

It is found in the Scriptures,

Written for me and for you.

Keep God's word securely within.

All our hope is only found in Him.

Romans 15:4

For whatever was written in earlier times was
written for our instruction, that through
perseverance and the encouragement of the
Scriptures we might have hope.

Be like David. He encouraged himself in the Lord
when he felt hopeless.

Even though the sky was full of clouds and the sun was not shining, I concluded that yes, the sun is shining. I just cannot see it. Then I realized that it would be totally dark if indeed there was no sunshine. We have days like that. A storm is brewing in our hearts, circumstances are out of our control, a myriad of other rough patches are making clouds in our days. But just like the sun is always shining, God is still shining in our life.

The Sun is Always Shining

The sun is always shining,

Even on a cloudy day.

We just can't see it

Because the clouds are in the way.

It would be totally dark,

And nothing would we see.

But there is a lesson

For both you and me.

Life can be full of cloudy days,

This we know.

But the Lord promises to be with us,

Wherever we may go.

Just like the sun is always there,

So is our Father too.

Don't lose heart or give up,

He is always there for you.

Joshua 1:9

Have I not commanded you? Be strong and
courageous! Do not tremble or be dismayed, for the
Lord your God is with you wherever you go.

I was thinking what it would sound like if only good news were broadcasted night after night.

Good evening everyone. Thank you for joining us. There were some positive notes on the employment front today. People of all ages and races were added to the employment statistics. New people being hired means more money will be pumped into our economy. Credit card usage is also dropping as people are learning how addictive those cards can be.

On the health front, a possible cure has been found for disease X. Several reputable doctors have co-authored agreement about yes, miracles have been documented all over the world.

The makers of a popular mid-sized automobile have put out a recall. No, it is not what you think. This recall is to install floor pads that will help the driver have a more enjoyable long-distance trip. Listen to this: no additional costs to the consumer. The company is using its end of the quarter profits to fund this recall.

The weather has certainly been a top news item of late. All the heavy rain has washed away many of the pollutants that have made breathing exceedingly difficult for many people, especially children and the elderly. Umbrella sales have skyrocketed.

Millions of dollars have been given to Haiti to rebuild its cities after going through some devastating natural occurrences. Volunteers from all over the world are coming together to share in the rebuilding efforts.

Finally, a story out of Washington, D.C. Would you believe that our representatives will be discussing bringing prayer and daily devotions into our public schools? Stay tuned for updates.

Thank you for watching. Join us the next time as we continue reporting the good news happening in our country and around the world.

Luke 4:18-19

The Spirit of the Lord is on me, because he has anointed me to preach good news to the poor. He has sent me to proclaim release to the captives and recovery of sight to the blind, to set free the oppressed, to proclaim the year of the Lord's favor.

I was in the grocery store recently just to pick up a few items. As I walked in the beverage aisle I was fascinated by the varieties of water on the shelves: purified, spring, flavored, filtered, and distilled. Who would have thought choosing water to drink would be such a chore? I am glad that those who know Jesus have the Holy Spirit as our source of Living Water, the only water that satisfies. (And it's free!)

Water in the Desert

Water in the desert

Gives a wearied soul hope,

Especially when one is

At the end of her rope.

Do you need to see water

In your desert today?

Have obstacles of life

Gotten in your way?

Are you thirsty

For the Living Water

That quenches all thirst?

To receive it

Jesus Christ must be put first.

He is also the Bread of Life.

The One who gives us strength

To rise above the strife.

Whatever desert

You are walking through,

Remember Jesus Christ

Promises to be with you.

John 4:13-14

Jesus said, "Everyone who drinks from this water
will get thirsty again. But whoever drinks from the
water that I will give him will never get thirsty again.
In fact, the water I will give him will become a well
of water springing up in him for eternal life."
Have you offered anyone a drink of the Living
Water?

I was driving down a busy street on my way to work. I saw a middle age woman in a wheelchair. She had just crossed one street and was waiting to cross another. I was touched by her courage. It was not easy maneuvering that wheelchair up on the sidewalk. I was thinking that it took a lot of will and stamina to do what she probably had to do every morning and every afternoon. I came to this conclusion because she rolled up to the bus stop where other people were waiting.

Inspired

I saw you in a wheelchair

Waiting to cross the street.

I thought how brave you had to be

With each obstacle you meet.

You were at a busy intersection

Full of speeding cars.

May God always keep you safe,

No matter where you are.

I hope I have the courage

I saw in you this day,

Offering no excuses,

As I go along my way.

Numbers 6:24-26

May the Lord bless you and protect you; may the Lord make his face shine on you and be gracious to you; may the Lord look with favor on you and give you peace.

When was the last time someone showed you some kindness? When was the last time you were kind to someone? Doesn't it feel good when either scenario happens? It could be a sincere word that turns a hard day into a better one. Perhaps an act of thoughtfulness that lifts someone's heavy load. Just your presence beside a friend could mean so much. Our Father can give us many ideas on how to show kindness, whether to a friend, family member or even a stranger.

Kindness

Speaking kind words

is a sign of love

Created for us to use

by our Father above.

Showing kindness and love

is our special part.

It may help to put a light

inside someone's heart.

Keep your words and actions

pure and true.

May the kindness you share with others

Find its way back to you.

Ephesians 4:32

And be kind and compassionate to one another,
forgiving one another, just as in Christ God also
forgave you.

Create a list of kind actions you can do. Choose
someone who would be blessed by your kindness.

We are always hearing about the older generation teaching the younger generation. But I feel that this is a two way street. We can learn from each other. The grandparent-grandchild relationship is a perfect example. Hanging out together offers many opportunities for learning. Also, to me, being a grandparent is an opportunity for "do-overs." What do I mean? Those things we were remiss in doing or not doing for our children, we get to make up for it with our grandkids. This includes those lessons we may have been too busy to see. The following list includes the lessons I have learned so far.

1. It is okay to continually ask "why." As adults, we tend to feel too embarrassed to ask questions. We feel some kind of vulnerability. Not so with children. This is how they learn. Now I ask more questions because I am still learning too.

2. Face my fears. My grandson was on a high slide and as he is sitting there working up his nerves to go down, I heard him say, "I must face my fears." He was only five and this was his first attempt on the higher slide. I took his cue and reflected on some of my fears and decided right there to begin facing them one by one.

3. A playground is the perfect place to make new friends. It never ceases to amaze me how quickly children can be friendly to one another. We were at the park and within minutes my granddaughter was running around with the other children playing and laughing. You would have thought they had been friends for a long time. Adults are more guarded. I wonder how many friendships we have missed because of that.

4. Watching the same movie several times never gets old. You may have seen a movie already but your grandchild wants to see it over and over again. You know what? Through that child's eyes you see parts of the story you may not have seen before.

5. It is all right to forget because there is always someone around to remind you. Many times, one of the grandchildren will say, "Grandma, don't you remember when...?" Look at things from their perspective.

6. Our granddaughter was visiting during my recovery from an accident. Her grandfather had gone to the grocery store. We were sitting in the living room and she suddenly asked, "Grandma, are you babysitting me or am I babysitting you?"

Next time you have an opportunity to be around anyone, regardless of their age, be still and listen to hear what lesson you might learn.

James 1:19

My dear brothers and sisters, understand this:
Everyone should be quick to listen, slow to speak,
and slow to anger...

Notes

Everybody loves hearing stories about miracles. I think many miracles get overlooked because we are expecting drum rolls and bright lights. For me, a miracle can range from a nest of baby birds to a healing of someone's body, to that long-awaited job.

Miracles

Look for the miracles

In each of your days.

It may be what someone does

Or what someone might say.

We often overlook the miracles

Right before our eyes,

Thinking they can only be

Magnificent in size.

But miracles are happening

All over the place,

Including that warm smile

On a friendly face.

We need to open our hearts

So we may see

God's love is a miracle

Given to you and to me.

Job 5:9

He does great and unsearchable things, wonders
without number.
Start a list of miracles you have witnessed or
personally experienced.

Several years ago, I entered a contest. The prize was an ice cream party for all your neighbors. The requirement was to write how an ice cream party would impact your neighbors. I figured most people would write an essay. I thought writing a poem would give me an edge. Guess what? I won a party for 100 people. The ice cream company that sponsored the contest, supplied everything. We had a great time.

Ice Cream Tastes Better With Neighbors

I want to meet my neighbors.

Yes, I really do.

Some I already know,

But some of them are new.

There are several homes

On our cul-de-sac street.

Having an ice cream party

Would be a tasty treat.

We could enjoy

An evening in July,

Eating delicious ice cream

Sitting side by side.

You never know the friendships
That may begin that night.

All because we are eating

A bowl of creamy delight.

Talking and enjoying ice cream

Sounds like fun to me,

Especially if there's chocolate,

Vanilla, or even strawberry.

I am sure when the evening is over

We will look back and say

That ice cream party

Really made our day.

We will know each other better

And more apt to say hello

The next time we see one another

As we come and go.

We will not be strangers anymore

Which really will be nice.

For we had some delicious ice cream

That helped to break the ice.

Romans 15:2

Each one of us is to please his neighbor for his good,
to build him up.

Think of something you can do for one of your
neighbors. Ask the Lord to give you an open door to
share His love.

Notes

Today I received a call from a very dear friend. Just out of the blue she calls, and I am home. It was the middle of the day when I would normally be out. We have not seen one another in several years, but it is always easy to start talking as if it were only yesterday. Do you have a friend like that? Who comes to mind as you read this? Why don't you, just out of the blue, give that person a call? Believe me, it will make not only your friend's day, but yours as well.

Out of the Blue

Out of the blue,

Just the other day,

A surprising telephone call

Came my way.

It was a voice

I had not heard in a while.

I was filled with excitement,

Like a young child.

Catching up was easy to do,

Discussing the old

As well as the new.

Out of the blue was ordained

By the Father.

He did this for us,

Like no other.

When was your last

Just out of the blue?

Think about it.

I am sure you could name a few.

Proverbs 25:25
Good news from a distant land is like cold water to
a parched throat.

Make a list of people you would like to reconnect
with just out of the blue.

In recent weeks, I have spent a lot of time looking out my window. Who needs to watch television? There are scenarios going on that are way more interesting and certainly more peaceful than what is being shown on cable. There are main characters, a plot or two, and plenty of action. No need for violence.

Outside My Window

I am looking out my window.

Telephone wires run from pole to pole.

They make up a playground for the birds and squirrels.

The squirrels have more nerve than I do.

They race across those wires,

Balancing themselves so well.

They know they are safe from their enemies.

What is their lesson for me?

Think on things above, not the things on earth.

That is God's answer for balance.

Colossians 3:2

Set your mind on things above, not on earthly things.

Turn your concerns into prayers and give thanks to the Lord for what He will do.

Most homes probably have shoeboxes full of photographs. With the popularity of scrapbooking, those photos can be celebrated in a more festive way. It really is a journey down memory lane when time is taken to look at the pictures and remember. They help us to remember the many God moments in our lives. All the little add ons used in scrapbooking make the pictures works of art.

Picture Albums

Pictures in my albums can show the good old days.

Scrapbooking makes it fun in so many ways.

If the background is too busy, I can crop it all out.

My scissors can work magic;

of this there is no doubt.

Thumbing through the albums can be lots of fun,

Whether I have an hour, or if I am on the run.

Memories come flooding back, of days gone by.

Some will be funny, while others will make me cry.

I can have more good old days, it really is true.

Pictures remind me of things I once knew.

Psalm 77:11-12

I will remember the Lord's works; yes, I will remember your ancient wonders. I will reflect on all you have done and meditate on your actions.

What are you going to do with your shoebox of photographs?

We met in a local thrift shop. She was in town visiting her brother. We both had items in mind we were looking for. We began having a conversation and discovered some common interests. As the conversation continued, we realized we were both Christians. She told me her testimony which included a wise word from her pastor. He told her to "read the red" in her Bible. At first she didn't understand what he meant. Then when she opened her Bible, she realized whenever Jesus spoke, the words were printed in red. Reading those words will give us a window into knowing Him better.

Read the Red

Some Bibles have Jesus' words

Printed in red.

This helps us zero in on

What He has said.

When you want

To know Him more,

Reading His words

Can help for sure.

Meditating on what Jesus has said

Can be life changing,

Whether in black or in red.

Reading the Word is a

Valuable use of time.

It helps us to know

What is on Jesus' mind.

What is on His mind

Should be on ours too.

It is His Word that can guide us

In what we say or do.

Let reading the red be

A part of your day.

Be on the lookout

As God makes a way.

John 14: 23

Jesus answered, "If anyone loves me, he will keep my word. My Father will love him, and we will come to him and make our home with him."

Choose any passage in red. Meditate on it. Did you learn anything new about Jesus?

The seasons are opportunities to observe the works of God. Each one serves many purposes. The different seasons we encounter in our lives, also serve many purposes. Some of those seasons may be full of joys as well as pain. The Lord promises to be with us, never to leave us alone.

Seasons of Change

The seasons were given to help us with changes.

Look at how the Lord lovingly arranges

Each winter, spring, summer, and fall,

Our Father is in control of them all.

The changes in our lives are like that too.

Our Heavenly Father knows just what to do.

Welcome each change that comes your way.

For God has your back each day.

No matter the season, He holds your hand.

It is on His promises that we can stand.

So, embrace the changes that comes about.

Give God the praise with a mighty shout.

Genesis 8:22

As long as the earth endures, seedtime and harvest,
cold and heat, summer and winter, day and night
will not cease.

Daniel 2:21

He changes the times and seasons; he removes
kings and establishes kings. He gives wisdom to
the wise and knowledge to those who have
understanding.

I do not know how it got started, but I began noticing signs. There were a variety of them and could be found in many different places. Signs were found in windows of businesses, on car windows, and of course on billboards. Have you notice the one major sign you can count on seeing at sporting events? Yes, John 3:16. The best sign of all.

Signs in Windows

Now Hiring

Walk-ins Welcomed

No Vacancy

For Sale

Room for Rent

Beware of Dog

Open

Closed

Smoke Free

Help Wanted

Going out of Business

By Appointment Only

Major Credit Cards Accepted

No Soliciting

Free Cat to Good Homes

Vacancy

John 3:16

For God loved the world in this way: He gave his
one and only Son, so that everyone who
believes in him will not perish but have eternal life.
What verse would you highlight if you had an
audience?

Once again, I am in awe of God as the Creator. Watching snowflakes fall, I marvel at the fact that each one is unique. This reminded me about how unique and special the Lord made us to be. We are that important to Him. He wants the best for each of us. That can become a reality when we choose to do life His way and not our own.

Snowflake

I am like a snowflake,

Special and unique.

God created me

As His masterpiece.

Just like a snowflake

Is specifically designed,

God had a purpose,

When He had me in mind.

Resting in His love

Is His will for me.

Not just in this moment

But for all eternity.

Ephesians 2:10

For we are His workmanship, created in Christ Jesus for good works, which God has prepared ahead of time for us to do.

Think about this and say to yourself: I am special to the Father. There is only one me. He loves me very much.

Often, I see him when I am on my way to church or the library. He stands at a red light just as cars are coming off the interstate. When I see him, he has a sign. Where did he get the cardboard and magic marker? Sometimes he has his dog. Questions go through my mind every time I see him.

Somebody's Son

There he is again holding that sign.

"Down on my luck," it says.

He is standing at the intersection where

Drivers are waiting for the light to change.

He is a young man with an old beard.

His clothes are dirty,

Too baggy for his frame.

He is somebody's son.

He has been at this spot before.

There is a dog with him today.

The dog looks better than he does.

Can't he get help from his family,

Or has he burned those bridges?

Is he really down on his luck,

Or is this a ploy?

He is somebody's son.

Where does he go if it is raining or cold?

Drivers avoid looking at him.

You can almost hear doors being locked.

Hurry up light,

Change so we do not have to see him,

This young man who is somebody's son.

Proverbs 10:1

Solomon's proverb: A wise son brings joy to his father, but a foolish son, heartache to his mother.

If you see someone holding up a "help" sign, remember he or she has parents. Ask the Father to meet their needs, to reunite with family and most of all accept Jesus as their Lord and Savior.

I have been in many conversations over the years where I have heard people say, "someday." I know those words have also been spoken by me. As I thought about it, I realize what a trap they could be. Almost an obstacle to derail us from our purpose. Just taking a small step towards that dream could make all the difference. One step leads to another step. Before we know it, that "someday" is "today." Ask the Lord to guide your thinking.

Someday

"Someday," many of us have said.

It is about those dreams dancing in our heads.

Our hopes and desires have gone astray.

The pressures of life show up each day.

But "someday" is right in our face,

Let us take steps to find our place.

Revisit those dreams and map them out.

That is what dreaming is all about.

"Someday" may be words to keep us down.

But the word "today" has a much sweeter sound.

Psalm 143:8

Let me experience your faithful love in the morning,
for I trust in you. Reveal to me the way I should go.

What "someday" have you been dreaming about?
Take a step towards that dream today.

Isn't there something beautiful about a spider's web? Of course, it is not lovely when you walk into one. I was able to see a completed web before I got too close. Its hidden beauty is what tricks the unsuspected. This is a good analogy for the way deception works.

The Spider's Web

Attached to the pillars,

Strong white strands of lace,

Trapping unsuspecting guests,

Into the warm sunlight.

Trapping unsuspecting guests,

Into its silent entryway.

Will several more guests

Find themselves there?

It is like a doily made of fine lace.

Trapping unsuspecting guests.

Jeremiah 17: 9

The heart is more deceitful than anything else, and incurable, who can understand it?

When making important decisions, make sure your heart doesn't take over.

So often anxiety rises within us when the threat of a storm is looming. If we change our perspective, we can see the storm as evidence of God's awesome power. As illustrated in the scriptures, Jesus' power was fully displayed. The most wonderful thing to remember: He is still displaying that power today.

Stormy Weather

When a storm is brewing outside your door,

It is not just a storm, but so much more.

Look at it as a reminder of what God can do.

Remember the times the Lord came through.

Be still, Jesus did say.

What storms are you facing this day?

Are the clouds of despair overtaking you?

Do you worry and fret about what to do?

The counsel of others may guide you along,

But applying God's wisdom will make you strong.

Meditate on His word day after day.

Look to Him to make a way.

Mark 4:39

He got up, rebuked the wind, and said to the sea, "Silence! Be still." The wind ceased, and there was a great calm.

Name a storm you are facing. Remember past storms and how the Lord brought you through them. He will do the same again.

I was scheduled to take a treadmill stress test. I had one several years ago and it was not a pleasant experience. I had that memory clouding my enthusiasm for another one. Well, I did not get to the level the doctor was looking for. He ordered an angiogram to rule out any blockages. The following poem is the thank you I sent to the doctor and staff at the testing center.

Thank You

Angiogram, angiogram, here I come.

I am not sure this will be fun.

I arrived at the center right on time,

Despite the fact it was hard to find.

The staff at the front desk were sweet.

Then the rest of the team I did meet.

The doctor was waiting like he said he would.

His stature was impressive when he stood.

The procedure was explained clearly to me,

To check that my arteries were blockage free.

I have tiny veins for the IV to be placed,

Trying to keep my composure, seasoned with grace.

I was wheeled to the lab and the test began.

It was over quickly and went as planned.

The doctor gave me clearance and said to exercise.

I was relieved and had huge tears in my eyes.

The weight on my shoulders started to lift.

His words to me were like a Christmas gift.

Psalm 34:4, 7

I sought the Lord, and he answered me and rescued me from all my fears... The angel of the Lord encamps around those who fear him and rescues them.

What are you concerned about today? Talk to the Lord about it, looking to him to watch over you.

God, our Father, is an artist. He has created so many beautiful shades. It had been raining for a few minutes. Then the sun came back out. Whatever was in the air had been washed away. Everything looked so clean and refreshed. I was amazed at the various shades of green I was noticing. Brainstorming ideas is something I do when writing a poem. I started thinking about many of the green things in our world.

The Color Green

Our God is the Master Artist

Who loves the color green.

He uses it in many ways,

As our earthly eyes have seen.

There are a variety of bushes,

Short, tall, and dark green,

While the fruity lime,

Has a shiny, waxy sheen.

There is the green frog

Croaking in the lake.

Hopping away when he sees a green snake.

A hungry green lizard is looking

For something to munch.

Anything smaller than him

Would make a great lunch.

Deep green emeralds are highly prized,

Gemstones, beautiful to the eyes.

There are more green things

Found all over,

Including many sprigs of clover.

Thank You, Lord, for the color green.

Jeremiah 17:7-8

The person who trusts in the Lord, whose
confidence indeed is the Lord, is blessed. He will be
like a tree planted by water; it sends its roots out
toward a stream, it doesn't fear when heat comes,
and its foliage remains green.

What is your favorite color? How has the
Father used it in His creation?

I had just picked up my granddaughter from school. I decided to take a different route home. As we were going down a sparsely populated street, my granddaughter saw a house on a hill and said in a sad little voice, "That house looks lonely, Grandma." I took a quick glance and had to agree with her. As we continued our drive, we talked about the difference between a lonely looking house and a home. The following poem is a result of that conversation.

The Lonely House

There on a hill stands a lonely house.

No other buildings are nearby.

It is alone in so many ways.

There are several windows,

but no one is looking out.

No flowers or bushes are part of the landscape.

A mailbox is nowhere to be seen.

No colorful swing set or sandbox

graces the backyard.

Not even a bird feeder hangs

from the nearby oak tree.

Weeds can be seen growing between

the cracks in the driveway.

This will remain a lonely house on a hill

Until a family makes it their home.

Psalm 127:1

Unless the Lord builds a house, its builders labor
over it in vain.

How would you describe your home?

I love mirrors. There is a mirror in each room in my house. Decorating books tell us that mirrors add depth to a room. As I passed by one recently, I stopped to look in the mirror. I took a moment to reflect on what I saw. The following poem is the result.

The Mirror

When I look in the mirror,

Who do I see?

Is it a reflection of Jesus,

Or is it still me?

More like Him I want to be,

So, when I look in the mirror,

I will not see me.

2 Corinthians 4:16

Therefore, we do not give up. Even though our outer person is being destroyed, our inner person is being renewed day by day.

2 Corinthians 3:18

We all, with unveiled faces, are looking as in a
mirror at the glory of the Lord and are being
transformed into the same image from glory to
glory; this is from the Lord who is the Spirit.
As you look in your mirror today, thank the Lord for
the changes He has been bringing into your life to
conform you to His image.

Perhaps you have been better at this than I. But have you seen a penny on the ground and just skipped over it thinking, it is only a penny? But on this day, as I was walking towards my car in a parking lot, I saw a lowly penny on the ground. In the past, I would have left it there, but for some reason I picked it up and dropped it in the armrest when I got into the car. I started thinking, from now on I am not going to leave free money on the ground. One thought led to another. That is how I ended up writing this poem. Also, I will carry tissue with me so I can safely pick the coin up.

The Penny Hunt

I found a shiny penny just the other day.

Often in the past I would have looked away.

It is only a penny, someone would say to me.

But it is still money and it is absolutely free.

When there are fifty, I can fill a roll.

Collecting more and more will be my goal.

I will look at my rolls often as they pile up high.

Wondering when I get enough, what will I buy?

The penny is more important to me now.

Every time I find one, I am sure I will say "wow!"

The pennies that I gather will help a roll to fill.

Enough of them together,

may pay an unexpected bill.

I look at these coins with a new respect,

Filled with excitement the more I collect.

A penny is still worth one cent, it is true,

but saving has always been a smart thing to do.

Luke 15:8-10

Or what woman who has ten silver coins, if she
loses one coin, does not light a lamp, sweep the
house, and searches carefully until she finds it?
When she finds it, she calls her friends and
neighbors together, saying, "Rejoice with me,
because I have found the silver coin I lost! I tell you,
in the same way, there is joy in the presence of
God's angels over one sinner who repents."

Do you have a stash of coins saved for a rainy day?

The Lord helps us not to be bored. Just look around and take in the surroundings. He has allowed me to witness a variety of activity just outside my door. From the different colors that dot the landscape to the wildlife creatures, there is always something to learn and find enjoyment in the moment. The Lord shows us more of Himself as we observe his handiwork.

The Robin

There is a robin on a wire.

What does he see?

Sometimes I think he is watching me.

Up on that wire he can look all around.

His head goes to the side and it also goes down.

The robin flies off and comes back again.

It is like he is playing a game and wants to win.

There is no price I could pay for this.

I wonder what other episodes I have missed.

Matthew 6:26

Consider the birds of the sky; they don't sow or reap or gather into barns, yet your heavenly Father feeds them. Aren't you worth more than they?

Do you need to be reminded of your worth? Meditate on what Christ Jesus did for you on the cross and how He is making intercession for us before the Father.

I enjoy watching people, wondering what they are thinking; what they may be feeling. We have a café at my church. I was sitting off in a corner eating a snack before the service. As I sat there, I began watching people come and go. It was interesting to view the different dynamics that took place. I saw a couple of individuals who did not look to the right nor to the left. I could tell they really did not want to be bothered. There were other facial expressions and tones in people's voices. I went home after the service and penned this poem, based on some assumptions I made.

A Hurting Heart

Why do I pretend all is well,

when deep down I am going through hell?

Do I really want to cry, but laugh instead,

to avoid facing the pain that's in my head?

I hide behind busyness or lots of TV,

to cloud those pictures, I don't want to see.

Avoiding the telephone when it rings,

keeping to myself, I do not say a thing.

The longer I ignore the pain that I feel, the greater

the time it will take to heal.

The Lord is near the brokenhearted; and he saves those crushed in spirit.

What has you weighed down today?

Grandmother, Times are A-Changing

As I think about my maternal grandmother, I often wonder what dreams she had as a young woman. Since I grew up in my grandparent's home, I had a front row seat to her life. The women of her generation were full time homemakers. Each day of the week was designated as a particular "chore" day. For example, Mondays were for laundry, Tuesdays for ironing, and so forth. Of course, fixing three meals, doing some light cleaning, and other daily chores were sprinkled throughout the day too.

Due to my grandmother's skill at saving money, we were able to purchase a black and white television set. That really opened a new world for both my grandmother and me. From the commercials you could tell who spent time watching television during the day. There were many laundry detergent ads along with the variety of quiz shows like, <u>Strike it Rich</u>, <u>The Price is Right and Beat the Clock.</u> During the evening programming, we saw commercials for cars and cigarettes. I also remember Perry Como encouraging viewers "to keep those letters coming."

The television gave my grandmother a welcome reprieve from the day to day operations of keeping house. As a little girl, it showed me that I could grow up to be a secretary, portrayed by Ann Southern, a switchboard operator like Vi on the same program or a teacher, like <u>Our Miss Brooks</u> Those were my role models.

Observing my grandmother's hard work ethic, her budgeting strategies, being a good steward of the family's possessions, and having a sense of pride on raising a healthy family are the values I took from her life. She was an incredibly wise woman.

Fast forward fifty years. Now I am a grandmother. What is my granddaughter observing about my life? It is nothing like her great-grandmother's life. That is for sure. Housework has never really been my cup of tea. Ironing? Only if I did not get that shirt out of the dryer in time.

My granddaughter will have so many choices. It is mind boggling to think about her future. But hopefully she will remember that I took advantage of opportunities that came my way or went out searching for them. She will recall that my mind and hands were always busy creating something or trying to figure things out. She will probably smile as she remembers that grandma never met a stranger. People are especially important to me and I really try to treat each person with respect. Even though she will have many more career choices, hopefully my granddaughter will take on some of my values as I have taken on some of my grandmother's.

Just like the black and white television set brought the outside world into my grandmother's life, for me it was the computer. Who would have thought such an invention would change how we communicate and get information? I cannot even begin to imagine what high powered inventions will be available to my granddaughter. I wonder what her automobile will be able to do.

Even something like cash. Now we have credit cards, debit cards, electronic transfer, etc. Cash as we know it is almost obsolete. What methods of financial transactions will she be using?

What would my grandmother say about all these changes? Changes are exciting but also scary. Sometimes I think we are moving, improving too rapidly. Did not some wise person say, "slow down, stop, take a moment to smell the roses?" I believe that advice will be worth following for many generations to come.

Proverbs 31:10

Who can find a wife of noble character? She is far more precious than jewels.

I am a people watcher. Often when I see someone, especially when they are alone, I wonder what are their dreams, what circumstances might be causing obstacles, what successes have they experienced, and more. What a difference our lives would be if we did see people through the Father's eyes.

Through Your Eyes

Help me, Father, to see people

Through Your eyes today.

Help me watch the things I do,

As well as the things I say.

Each person I meet

Has their own stories to tell.

All the more reason

I should treat each person well.

I do not know

What someone is going through.

They may be perplexed,

Not knowing what to do.

Show me, Father,

The part I should play.

I do not know what they need,

But I know I can pray.

Help me to see people

Through Your eyes today,

Knowing You are the One,

Who can make a way.

Mark 6:34

When he went ashore, he saw a large crowd and
had compassion on them, because they were like
sheep without a shepherd.

When was the last time you looked at someone
through the Father's eyes?

Gently loved, previously used, preowned, flea markets, thrift stores, consignment shops—these are all code words for getting rid of our stuff. In the past, we had secondhand stores but now we have elevated the market.

I enjoy shopping for treasures, and I must say some have been found over the years. I keep a list of things I am looking to find. Of course, I find things that were not on my list and that makes the trip even more exciting.

As I make my way up and down the aisles, I am overwhelmed with the volume of merchandise. Going into stores like these begs the question: Why do we have so much stuff? Riding through town, one will see several storage places. Also, even though people have garages, their cars are always parked in the driveway. Perhaps there is stuff stored in the car's place?

Luke 12:15

He then told them, watch out and be on guard against all greed, because one's life is not in the abundance of his possessions.

Notes

It was just a normal day with a variety of errands to complete. I began to realize I was doing more waiting than anything else. Using a clipboard I always carry, I started making a list of the times spent waiting. Most of the waiting was the result of other people's actions, not so much my own. I decided to use those nuggets of time to pray.

Waiting

Do you realize how much

Waiting we do?

I am sure it is the same

For me as it is for you.

We wait in line to cash a check,

Where it takes longer than we expect.

At the doctor's office we wait too,

Wondering what she will do.

We wait for the green light so we can go.

Then realize there is a reason traffic is slow.

There was an accident up ahead.

Now more waiting my inner voice said.

Waiting seems to be a part of each day.

We can use that time to pray, pray, pray.

Lamentations 3:25-26

The Lord is good to those who wait for him, to the person who seeks him. It is good to wait quietly for salvation from the Lord.

Make a list today of your waiting times. Use them as opportunities to pray.

I went to visit my daughter in the hospital. She had given birth to our first grandson the day before. As I approached the entrance, a large stone-covered receptacle caught my attention. There were several cigarette butts in the sand. The way they were position looked like a piece of abstract sculpture. Various shades of lipsticks were represented. Some were crushed, while others were twisted and just thrown haphazardly into the sand. Half were barely smoked while some had been smoked all the way down.

This picture stayed in my mind for several days. The more I wondered the more questions I had: If each cigarette could talk, what would it tell me about the person? Was it an employee who needed a break? Could it have been someone who had received a life changing diagnosis? Or perhaps a new dad who had witness the birth of his son?

I did find it ironic these small white tobacco-filled tubes, which are known to cause illness, would be seen outside the doors of a hospital.

A few months later, I went back to that hospital to visit a friend. The receptacle had been replaced with a trash bin. No places for used cigarettes. A sign was on display stating it was a "smoke free" area. I guess someone else found it a little ironic also.

My question now, where are the people who would have been outside smoking? Where do they go to handle their stressful moments? Perhaps the chapel inside the hospital was being used a little more often. This would certainly be a healthier alternative.

1 Peter 5:7

...casting all your care on Him because He cares for you.

Barbara Karen Hodges grew up in a small New Jersey town. Reading and writing were her favorite things to do. She had access to a great library and spent a lot of time there.

After graduating from high school, she attended college and earned a Bachelor of Arts degree in elementary education. Barbara taught school for several years. After retiring, she worked part time as a circulation assistant at her local library. That was her dream job, to be surrounded by books and to interact with others who also loved to read.

As time went on, Barbara realized that she had a desire to write a book. A time came when all the pieces fell into place for her dream to become a reality. With encouragement from family and friends she started putting this book together.

Barbara's faith in the Lord is very important to her. She wants her writing to reflect her relationship with Him. She desires to point others to Him.

Her newest hobby is participating in craft fairs. She creates bookmarks, memo pads, and magnets displaying her original poetry.

She has three adult daughters, eight grandchildren, and one great grandson.